A NOTE TO PARENTS

When your children are ready to "step into reading," giving them the right books—and lots of them—is as crucial as giving them the right food to eat. **Step into Reading Books** present exciting stories and information reinforced with lively, colorful illustrations that make learning to read fun, satisfying, and worthwhile. They are priced so that acquiring an entire library of them is affordable. And they are beginning readers with an important difference—they're written on four levels.

Step 1 Books, with their very large type and extremely simple vocabulary, have been created for the very youngest readers. **Step 2 Books** are both longer and slightly more difficult. **Step 3 Books,** written to mid-second-grade reading levels, are for the child who has acquired even greater reading skills. **Step 4 Books** offer exciting nonfiction for the increasingly proficient reader.

Children develop at different ages. **Step into Reading Books,** with their four levels of reading, are designed to help children become good—and interested—readers *faster*. The grade levels assigned to the four steps—preschool through grade 1 for Step 1, grades 1 through 3 for Step 2, grades 2 and 3 for Step 3, and grades 2 through 4 for Step 4—are intended only as guides. Some children move through all four steps very rapidly; others climb the steps over a period of several years. These books will help your child "step into reading" in style!

For Poppy, who started it all—S.A.K.

Cover photographs: Leviton-Atlanta/*Sports Illustrated* (H. Aaron); Corbis/Bettmann (T. Williams); John Biever/*Sports Illustrated* (S. Sosa); Mitch Blank Archives/Archive Photos (B. Ruth); © Major League Baseball Photos (T. Cobb); Chris Trotman/Duomo (M. McGwire).

Interior photographs: AP/Wide World Photos, p. 28; Bettmann, p. 30; Corbis/ASP, p. 41; Foundation for the Tri-State Community, Inc., p. 38; V. J. Lovero/*Sports Illustrated*, p. 43; Brad Mangin/Duomo, p. 44; National Baseball Library and Archive, Cooperstown, N.Y., p.13, 14, 16, 21, 22, 27, 33; Reuters/Tim Parker/Archive Photos, p. 47.

New Edition

Text copyright © 1995, 2000 by S.A. Kramer
Illustrations copyright © 1995 by Jim Campbell
All rights reserved under International and Pan-American Copyright Conventions.
Published in the United States by Random House, Inc., New York, and simultaneously in Canada by Random House of Canada Limited, Toronto. Originally published in different form by Random House, Inc., in 1995.

www.randomhouse.com/kids

Library of Congress Cataloging-in-Publication Data
Kramer, Sydelle, Baseball's greatest hitters / by S. A. Kramer ; illustrated by Jim Campbell.
p. cm. — (Step into reading. A step into sports step 4 book)
ISBN 0-375-80583-4 (trade) — ISBN 0-375-90583-9 (lib. bdg.)
1. Baseball players—United States—Biography—Juvenile literature. 2. Batting (Baseball)—Juvenile literature. [1. Baseball players.]
I. Campbell, Jim, 1942– ill. II. Title. III. Series: Step into reading. Step 4 book.
GV865.A1K73 1995 796.357—dc20 [B] 94-16497

Printed in the United States of America March 2000 14 13 12 11 10 9 8 7 6 5

STEP INTO READING, RANDOM HOUSE, and the Random House colophon are registered trademarks and the Step into Reading colophon is a trademark of Random House, Inc.

BASEBALL'S GREATEST HITTERS

By S. A. Kramer
Illustrated by Jim Campbell

Random House 🏠 New York

The Hardest Job in Sports

Batter up. The pitcher delivers. It's a fast-ball, steaming in at more than 90 miles per hour. The ball reaches the plate in less than half a second. The hitter must react in the blink of an eye. Should he swing? Is the pitch a strike or a ball? Will it hit him, causing serious injury?

To make the right decision, the batter must concentrate completely. After all, the bat must connect with an object only 2.868 inches wide. No wonder some feel hitting is the hardest job in sports.

Of course, great hitters do more than just get the bat on the ball. They swing with power and drive in run after run. When the game's on the line, they're the players who always come through.

There have been great hitters ever since baseball began. But in the early days the game was different. The ball was heavier, so it didn't carry very far. Pitchers could spit on it or scrape it, getting it wet and dirty. As the innings passed, the ball grew hard to see. Unlike today, the umpire didn't toss it from the field.

That time in baseball is known as the "Dead Ball Era." Hitters didn't clobber many homers because of the wet, dirty, heavy ball. But in 1920, teams began to use a light, clean, dry ball. A player named Babe Ruth started slamming home runs, and the game was changed forever. Now the greatest batters are usually sluggers. And fans love to argue about who's the best.

Keep in mind not all the top hitters played in the major leagues. Before 1947, African Americans were not allowed in the majors. Some of our most spectacular athletes were in the Negro leagues.

So, who are baseball's greatest hitters? Forget the fastest runners and the finest fielders. Not even the top all-around players count. This book is just about true heroes of the bat.

1
The Man Who Had to
Be the Best

Detroit, 1912. Three men are trying to mug Tiger star Ty Cobb. But Ty battles back. He's not about to let himself be robbed.

Ty's a fighter, even when he's playing ball. He's been known to climb into the stands and slug a fan who's booed him. Once when he was heckled, he threw his bat into the seats. He shouts at umpires and spikes fielders guarding the bases. Many players think Ty is insane.

But now he is fighting for his life. One of the men has a knife. He stabs Ty in the back, and blood pours from the five-inch wound.

That just makes Ty angrier. He starts to punch fast and hard. Two of the men flee, but Ty chases the third down. He hits him so many times, he believes he's killed him.

Ty's own wound is serious, yet he refuses to see a doctor. Wearing a homemade bandage, he plays the next day. Blood soaks the dressing, but Ty slams a double and a triple. Not even a stabbing can stop him.

Ty would always do anything to succeed. "I've got to be first—in everything," he said. He didn't just slide into a base, he flew spikes-first at a fielder. Players knew he'd

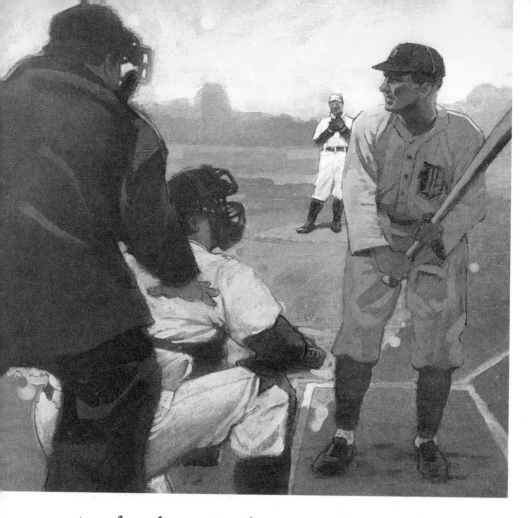

try for the extra base, so they rushed their throws and made errors.

But it was pitchers who feared Ty the most. He did whatever he could think of to annoy them. On deck, he would grit his teeth, swinging three bats at a time. With his hooked nose and small eyes, he looked mean.

When he walked to the plate, he'd often

shout out an insult. Sometimes he'd bend over and shake his rear end at the pitcher. Once, at bat, he kept his back to the mound. The confused hurler fired four balls in a row.

Ty could hit any pitch, so no one was sure what to throw him. He always choked up on his short bat, hands apart on the handle. His knees bent slightly as he held the bat away from his body.

A tricky hitter, Ty did what no one expected. But he always made contact with the ball. Since he played mostly in the Dead Ball Era, he rarely belted homers. Still, he drove in run after run and was probably the best bunter ever.

By 1925, everyone wanted to be a slugger. That's when Ty pulled one of the greatest batting feats ever. He announced he would "for the first time...be deliberately going for home runs." To prove he could hit homers if he wanted to, he smacked three in one game and two in the next.

Ty performed feats few players could. His lifetime batting average is the highest in history: .366. Games were more exciting when he was in them—he'd get a single, steal second, and score on an infield out.

But Ty could be selfish. If he was in a slump, he'd stay on the bench to protect his average. When he didn't get his way, he threw terrible tantrums. Once he refused to play because he didn't like his hotel room.

Throughout his life, Ty had very few friends. He was prejudiced against African Americans and seemed more concerned about money than people. Even as an 18-year-old rookie, he couldn't get along with his teammates.

Baseball was the most important thing in his life. As a boy, he wanted to play so badly, he sewed his own glove and carved his own bat. Because his father disapproved, he wrote in secret to arrange tryouts. Once

in the majors, he worked hard to learn all he could about hitting.

By the time Ty grew old, he was bitter, lonely, and rich. Only three baseball people came to his funeral. Though unpopular to the end, he was still considered a legend. "To see him," one player said, "was to remember him forever."

TYRUS RAYMOND (TY) COBB

(The Georgia Peach)

1886–1961	Left-handed
6'1", 175 lbs.	Outfielder

Lifetime batting average: .366

Lifetime slugging average: .512

Career: 1905–1928, mostly with the Detroit Tigers

Hall of Fame

• Great Feats •

- Has the highest lifetime batting average.
- Has the second most lifetime hits (4,191).
- Is first in runs scored (2,246).
- Is second in triples (295) and fourth in doubles (724).
- Is fourth in stolen bases (891) and fifth in RBIs (1,937).
- Is fourth in total bases (5,854) and eighth in extra-base hits (1,136).
- Batted over .300 for 23 years (over .400 three times) and won 10 American League batting titles.
- Is seventh in on-base percentage—.433, with nine 200-hit seasons.
- Was the youngest to win a batting crown (he was 20 in 1907, and hit .350), and the youngest to ever get 1,000 hits.

• Greatest Feat •

- In 1911, he batted .420, with 127 RBIs, 147 runs scored, 248 hits, and 83 stolen bases—one of the greatest seasons ever.

2
The First Slugger

It's the third game of the 1932 World Series. The New York Yankees are in Chicago to face the Cubs. The score is tied in the top of the fifth inning when Yankee slugger Babe Ruth comes out on deck.

Babe is baseball's first power hitter. By clouting homer after homer, he has changed the game more than anyone else. But he's 37 now. Is he too old to hit anymore? Babe, however, still believes in himself.

Cub fans boo as Babe steps into the batter's box. Players on the Cub bench heckle him. When the first pitch is a strike, some shout "Baboon! Potbelly!" Babe, who is overweight, grins and raises one finger.

For years he's had trouble keeping himself in shape. He won't exercise like his teammates, or follow a diet. For breakfast he eats 18-egg omelets. Six hot dogs and six sodas make up a snack. At dinner he wolfs down two whole fried chickens.

The next two pitches are balls. But the third is a strike. The fans scream and yell. A Cub shouts: "You're just a tramp!"

Will Babe strike out? He does go after a lot of bad pitches. He never chokes up on the bat, and he always takes a big swing. He tries to sock the ball so hard that he some-times spins around when he misses. But mostly he connects. Babe can homer on a pitch just above his shoes. He can whack a ball so low and hard, he fears one day he'll kill a pitcher.

Babe rubs some dirt on his hands. He looks at the Cub dugout and raises two fingers—he's down two strikes, but there's one left to go. Babe says aloud, "It only takes one to hit it." Some people think he points to the center-field bleachers.

Deep in the batter's box, Babe gets ready.

The pitcher fires. It's a change-up, low and away. Babe swings his heavy bat—the ball rockets into the sky. It goes over the center-field wall. Home run!

Babe circles the bases, laughing. "You lucky bum!" he says to himself. As he rounds third, he clasps his hands over his head. He ignores the garbage the fans are throwing on the field.

The Yankees win this game, and then the Series. Babe's at-bat becomes one of the most famous ever. His legend grows all the greater.

Yet even before that clout, Babe was the best-known American in the world. For years crowds followed him wherever he went. Stadium attendance tripled for games he played in.

Before Babe, a player could hit just 10 homers, yet lead the league. Then in 1919, Babe slammed 29. The rest of his team managed only four. This feat seemed even greater since Babe was best known as a pitcher.

In 1920, he became a full-time outfielder. That year he hammered 54 home runs. That wasn't just more than any other player—it was more than any American League *team*.

Yet when he was young, no one felt he would amount to much. By the age of eight, he was cutting classes, stealing, and chewing tobacco. He had to be put in reform school.

Babe was always in trouble, but he was also generous and kind. In school he bought candy for the small boys and took the blame for their pranks. People didn't seem to notice he was ugly—they just saw his joyful smile. After he became famous, he visited sick children in the hospital. Time after time he would leave $100 behind.

When he died at 53, the whole world mourned. No man was more a baseball hero than Babe.

GEORGE HERMAN (BABE) RUTH
(The Sultan of Swat, The Bambino)

1895–1948	Left-handed
6'2", 215 lbs.	Pitcher, outfielder

Lifetime batting average: .342

Lifetime slugging average: .690

Career: 1914–1935, mostly for the Boston Red Sox

and the New York Yankees

Hall of Fame

• Great Feats •

• First in lifetime slugging average, with the highest single-season slugging average (.847 in 1920).

• Was the greatest run-producer ever—drove in a run every 3.79 times at bat.

• Is first in home run percentage (8.50). This means he hit more home runs in his number of times at bat than anyone else.

• In 1921, he had the most total bases (457) and the most extra-base hits (119) of any single season.

• Is first in total walks (2,056), with the most in a single season (170 in 1923).

• Has the second most runs scored (177 in 1921).

• Is second in runs (2,174, tied with Hank Aaron), homers (714), RBIs (2,213), and on-base percentage (.474).

• Is third in total extra-base hits (1,356), and fifth in total bases (5,793).

• Hit over 50 homers four times and batted .300 or better 17 times, including .393 in 1923.

• Greatest Feat •

• In 1921, he batted .378, with 59 homers, 171 RBIs, 177 runs scored, 44 doubles, 16 triples, 144 walks, 17 stolen bases, and a slugging average of .846—a display of power never equaled.

3
The Last .400 Hitter

September 28, 1941. The Boston Red Sox have come to Philadelphia to play the Athletics. There's a doubleheader scheduled, but the fans are interested in something else. They've come to watch Ted Williams bat.

Ted is only 23, but he's hitting .3995. More than anything, he wants to bat .400.

Today is the last day of the season. If he doesn't play, his average will be rounded up to .400. But he takes the field—he wants to prove he can really do it.

Ted has been feeling the pressure—his average has dropped 13 points in the last 12 games. Just last night, he walked 10 miles, worrying.

The Philadelphia crowd is rooting for the Red Sox slugger. Even some of the Athletics wish him luck. As he comes to the plate, the umpire tells him to relax. But Ted is so nervous, his hands are shaking.

He steps into the batter's box and keeps his feet wide apart. Wiggling his hips and shoulders, he jiggles up and down. He swings his light bat and twists his strong hands around its handle. He's fussy about his bats—once he returns one because the handle is off just five thousandths of an inch.

Ted stares at the pitcher. He's concentrating completely. When the ball shoots in, he strides confidently forward. With perfect timing, he swings and connects.

It's a drive down the first-base line. The crowd hopes it's a hit. When it falls in for a single, they cheer Ted on.

Next time up he homers. Then he gets two more singles. He's batting .404 now, but still he won't sit down. He's going to play the whole doubleheader. He wants everyone to know he's truly a great hitter.

The fans roar each time he comes to the plate. He gets two more hits, one a line drive blasted so hard that it dents an outfield loudspeaker.

By the end of the day, Ted is batting .406. He finishes the season first in average,

homers, walks, runs scored, slugging average, and on-base percentage. All his years of
practice have finally paid off.

Ted has always "wanted to be the greatest hitter who ever lived." He started playing baseball when he was six. At the age of 12, he spent most nights in his backyard, practicing hitting in the moonlight. His parents didn't stop him. They were rarely around. Ted was lonely, underweight, and tense— but he loved swinging a bat.

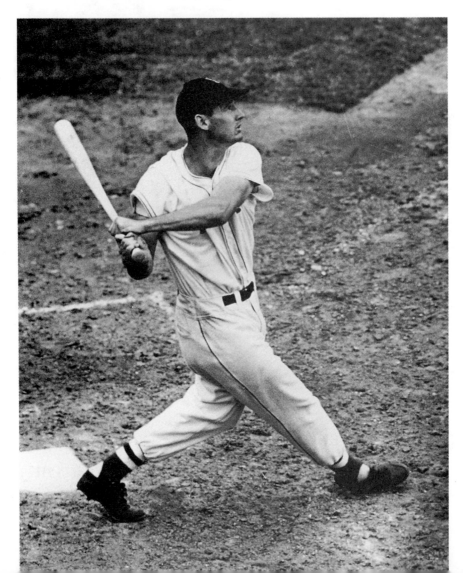

By the time he was 20, Ted was in the majors. He studied pitchers and umpires, becoming an expert on the strike zone. He knew the slope of each stadium's batter's box and the direction of the wind. Like a scientist, he researched how the ball moves to the plate.

Ted was baseball's most patient hitter. He rarely swung at pitches that weren't strikes. But some say he thought only of his average and didn't care about his team.

Ted wasn't easy to get along with. He threw tantrum after tantrum. At the ballpark, he hurled bats, ripped out pipes, and smashed lights. He spat at fans who booed him. To show he didn't care what people thought, he never tipped his cap to a cheering crowd. When he homered in his very last time at bat, he wouldn't acknowledge the applause.

As rude as Ted was, he could also be generous. From childhood on, he helped the sick

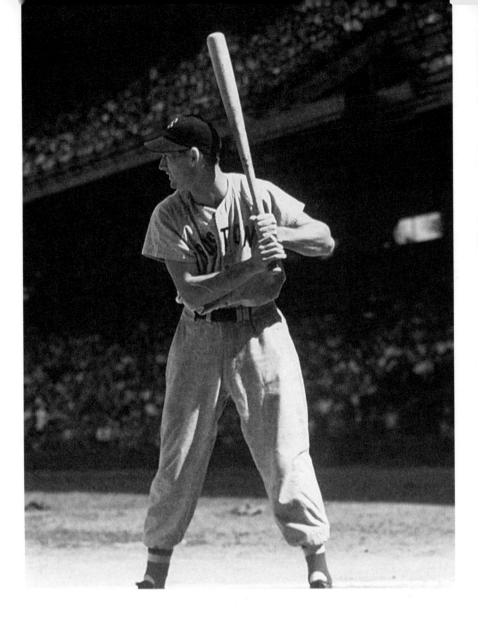

and the needy. He raised millions of dollars for a children's cancer hospital.

Hitting, though, was what he cared about most of all. Many who saw him play insist he was the greatest of all time.

THEODORE SAMUEL (TED) WILLIAMS

(The Kid, The Splendid Splinter)

1918–   Left-handed

6'3", 205 lbs.   Outfielder

Lifetime batting average: .344

Lifetime slugging average: .634

Career: 1939–1960, with the Boston Red Sox

Hall of Fame

• Great Feats •

• Has the highest lifetime on-base percentage (.483) and the highest single-season percentage (.551 in 1941).

• Is the only American Leaguer to win two triple crowns (first in league in RBIs, homers, and batting)—1942 and 1947.

• At 21, he had what may be the greatest rookie year ever (.327, 31 homers, 145 RBIs).

• Is second in lifetime slugging average and in walks (2,019).

• Is sixth in lifetime batting average.

• Led the league in batting average seven times and slugging average nine times.

• Led the league in walks eight times.

• Is the oldest player ever to win a batting championship (he was 40 in 1958, and hit .328).

• Set many records despite serving five years in the Navy at the height of his career.

• Greatest Feat •

• The last .400 hitter, he hit .406 in 1941, with 37 homers, 120 RBIs, 135 runs scored, 145 walks, a slugging average of .735, and an on-base percentage of .551. He struck out only 27 times that season.

4
Hammerin' Hank

Atlanta, April 8, 1974. Hank Aaron slowly walks to the plate. A hush falls over the jam-packed stadium. Over 50,000 fans are at this Braves-Dodgers game. Right now they all have their eyes fixed on Hank. Is tonight the night he'll break Babe Ruth's home-run record?

Some white people don't want Hank to outhit Babe. Because Hank is black, they don't feel he's Babe's equal. They mail letters that threaten him and his family. The FBI is brought in to investigate. Hank gets protection from a police bodyguard.

This isn't the first time that baseball has placed Hank in danger. When he began his career, some felt that whites and blacks shouldn't play on the same team. White fans jeered him. Some threatened to shoot him.

players called him terrible names. A few pitchers threw at him on purpose.

Their prejudice made Hank determined to succeed. He knew that the best way to show that blacks are equal was to play as well as he could. Controlling his anger, he kept swinging his bat. Because he was a quiet man, few fans noticed his achievements. But

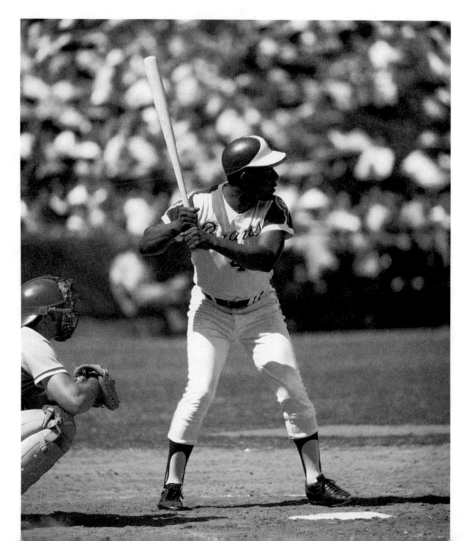

tonight he can prove he's a great player. He'll make history for himself and for all blacks.

It's the fourth inning. Hank stands in the back of the batter's box. The Dodger pitcher knows he must be careful—Hank can hit almost anything. It's especially hard to throw a fastball by him.

The pitch sails in. It's a change of pace, in the dirt. Hank doesn't swing—he's waiting for the right pitch. As usual, he seems calm. But the tension is building. It's as if everybody's holding their breath.

The pitcher delivers, but he's made a mistake. It's a slider down the middle. Hank can wallop this ball!

With perfect timing, Hank waits till the last second. Then he shifts all his weight to his front foot. With quick wrists, he whips the bat around. Fans hear the wood smack the ball.

It's a line drive. For an instant, Hank thinks the shortstop can catch it. But the ball speeds high and deep to left-center field. It shines like a comet in the stadium lights.

Will the left-fielder catch it? No—it sails over the fence! Hank has hit home run number 715. The record is his.

The crowd explodes in cheers. Hank starts to circle the bases. He feels as if everything is happening in slow motion. The Dodger first baseman reaches out and shakes his hand. Two college students race from the stands and pat him on the back as he rounds second.

At home plate, all his teammates congratulate him. They try to lift him onto their shoulders, but Hank won't let them. He wants to embrace his parents, who have come out onto the field. Later he says, "I never knew that my mother could hug so tight."

Hank begins to cry. He's both happy and relieved. "Thank God it's over," he says after the game.

Hank Aaron holds baseball's record for the most home runs and most runs batted in. Yet the greatness he achieved came only after years of struggle.

Born poor in Alabama, Hank often had no money to buy baseballs. So he made his own by rolling stockings around golf balls. Sometimes he batted crumpled tin cans.

At 18 he became a professional player,

even though his mother wanted him to teach school. He hit steadily and well, but few felt he was a true power hitter. He never showed emotion and didn't have a flashy style. Despite his excellence, there always seemed to be a bigger star.

But season after season, Hank produced runs. It was his consistency as a hitter that made him great. The record shows, as one writer said, that Hank was "the man who did the most with a baseball bat."

HENRY LOUIS (HANK) AARON
(Hammerin' Hank)

1934–   Right-handed

6', 180 lbs.   Outfielder

Lifetime batting average: .305

Lifetime slugging average: .555

Career: 1954–1976, mostly for the Milwaukee,

then the Atlanta, Braves.

Hall of Fame

• Great Feats •

• Is first in total homers (755), RBIs (2,297), total bases (6,856), and extra-base hits (1,477).

• Is third in total hits (3,771).

• Is second in runs scored (2,174, tied with Babe Ruth).

• Played in the third most games (3,298).

• Had 40 or more homers eight times.

• Had more than 100 RBIs 11 times.

• Hit .300 or better 14 times.

• Was the second youngest player to get 1,000 hits.

• Greatest Feat •

• Hank is one of only four players in history to get 3,000 hits, 300 homers, and 200 stolen bases.

5
Home Run Kings

St. Louis, Missouri, September 8, 1998. A sell-out crowd is watching the Cardinals play the Chicago Cubs. It's two out in the bottom of the fourth, and Cardinals' slugger Mark McGwire is at the plate. All 49,987 fans are on their feet. They want their red-headed hero to smash a home run. If he does, he'll break the most famous record in all of sports.

In 1961, New York Yankee Roger Maris slammed 61 homers in a single season. Yesterday Mark tied him, with 18 games left to go. Now, with one swing, he can become the first ever to wallop 62.

Crouched and pigeon-toed in the batter's box, Mark waves his bat around. It looks like a toothpick in his hands because he's so enormous. Six foot five, 250 pounds, he has arms as big as a person's head. He's so strong, his homers soar an average of 425 feet. One player says, "He's like Godzilla."

Mark waits for the first pitch. It's a low fastball, right down the middle. He takes his short, 80-mile-an-hour swing as hundreds of flashbulbs go off. Fans are taking photos in case it's the record-setting blast.

The ball shoots off the bat, a low liner that rockets to left field. Mark is not sure it will clear the eight-foot-high wall 341 feet away. Digging for first base, he keeps his eye on the ball. "The next thing I knew," he says, "the ball disappeared...I did it!"

Number 62! It's Mark's shortest homer of the year, but the most important. Fireworks light up the sky as the crowd goes wild. Mark's so excited, he misses first base and has to go back to touch it. When he crosses the plate, he lifts his 10-year-old son, the Cardinals' bat boy, high in the air. His teammates crowd around and he gives them all a hug.

Out in right field, Cub superstar Sammy Sosa is applauding. Just like Mark, he is chasing the home run record. But Sammy and Mark aren't rivals—instead, they cheer each other on. In one of baseball's greatest acts of sportsmanship, Sammy runs in from the outfield to hug Mark.

Both sluggers know the home run race is far from over. Mark hasn't finished homering yet, and neither has Sammy. Five days later, Sammy breaks Roger Maris's record, too.

Sammy's having one of the greatest baseball seasons ever. In the past, he was a wild swinger with as many strikeouts as hits. Fans would call him "Sammy So-so." But now he's learned to wait for a good pitch. In June 1998, he set the major-league record for most homers in one month—20.

Sammy's an emotional man who has fun on the field. He shows the more serious Mark how to relax and enjoy the fans' attention. Every time he hits a homer, he kisses two fingers, thumps his chest over his heart, and holds his fingers out in a V. That's Sammy's way of telling his mother he loves her.

Sammy says his life is "kind of like a miracle." That's because he's gone from terrible poverty to stardom and success. He was born into a poor family in the Dominican Republic. When he was seven, his father died. By the age of nine, Sammy had to work shining shoes, selling oranges, and washing cars.

He didn't start to play baseball until he was 14. Since he couldn't afford equipment, he used a tree branch for a bat, a rolled-up sock for a ball, and a milk carton for a glove. A talented athlete, he wanted to make it to the major leagues. He knew that then his family would never be poor again.

Sammy's plan worked. At 16, he was discovered by a major-league scout. When the Texas Rangers brought him to America, he didn't know any English. After cashing his first paycheck, Sammy brought the money back to his room. He spread it out on his bed and rolled happily around in it. Then he told his family that they were rich.

Now Sammy's an American citizen and a millionaire. But he's never forgotten his roots. He donates a lot of money to help the poor in his hometown. He's given so much away, kids there call him "Sammy Claus."

Mark had a very different life. He had a comfortable childhood in California. His father was a dentist. The family was athletic, so Mark always played sports. He wanted to be a pitcher, but he was a power hitter even at 10. That's when he had his first Little League at-bat—and smashed a home run!

Mark never took his talent for granted. He practiced hard to make himself better. A modest boy, he put his trophies in the closet instead of on display. Generous in spirit, he gave away his clothes, baseball gloves, even his shoes to kids who had less than he did.

After a successful college baseball career, Mark joined the Oakland Athletics. In 1987, he set the home run record for rookies by banging 49 round-trippers. Fans nicknamed him "Orange Crunch." He seemed like a player on his way to greatness.

But in 1991, Mark fell into a long slump. He batted only .201 and was booed constantly. He lost his confidence. He was injured. In 1996, he almost quit baseball.

But his love for the game brought him back, better than ever. Now Mark's so focused on baseball, he sometimes doesn't know what day it is. Still, his deepest feelings aren't for sports. His son is the most important thing in his life. Each year, Mark donates a million dollars to fight child abuse.

Mark finishes the season by hitting his 70th home run in his last at-bat. It's a record that may never be broken. Sammy hits 66 and leads the Cubs to the play-offs. He is named the National League's Most Valuable Player.

Together, Mark and Sammy are baseball's home run kings. But even more important, they've proven that nice guys finish first.

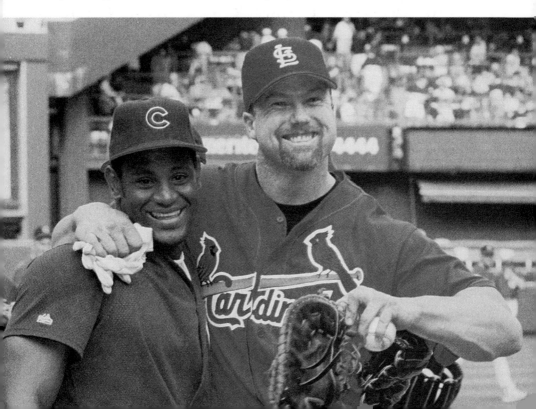

MARK DAVID McGWIRE
(Big Mac)

1963–   Right-handed
6'5", 250 lbs.   First baseman
Career: 1987– , for the Oakland Athletics
and the St. Louis Cardinals

• Great Feats •

• Hit the most homers by a rookie (49 in 1987).
• Is the first player to hit 30 or more homers in each of his first four seasons.
• Is the only player to hit 20 or more homers in both leagues in the same season.
• Is the only player to hit 20 or more homers for two teams in one season.
• Is the only player to hit 50 or more homers three years in a row.
• Highest career percentage of homers per times at bat (11.3).

• Greatest Feat •

• Has the most homers in a single season (70 in 1998).

SAMUEL SOSA Y PERALTA
(Slammin' Sammy)

1968–   Right-handed
6', 210 lbs.   Right fielder
Career: 1989– , for the Texas Rangers, the Chicago White Sox,
and the Chicago Cubs

• Great Feats •

• Has the second most homers in a single season (66 in 1998).
• Hit the most homers in one month (20 in June 1998).
• Is the only Cub ever to hit at least 30 home runs and steal at least 30 bases in a single season (1993, 1995).
• Has averaged 46 homers over the last three seasons.

• Greatest Feat •

• In 1998, he had one of the greatest single seasons in baseball history, hitting .308, with 66 home runs and 158 RBIs. He was named the National League's MVP.